ALL FOR DT

BARBARA HAGEN

To order additional copies of this book, contact:
Xlibris
844-714-8691
www.Xlibris.com
Orders@Xlibris.com

ISBN: Softcover   979-8-3694-0615-1
        Hardcover   979-8-3694-0616-8
        EBook   979-8-3694-0614-4
Library of Congress Control Number: 2023916158

Print information available on the last page

Rev. date: 08/21/2023

Contents

Part One: Poetry for God 1

    Jesus Set Us Free 2

    The Day That God Wept upon the Earth 3

    A Poem for My Savior and My King 5

    God Is Our Ray of Hope 6

    How Did You Keep Quiet? 7

    Beep! Judging Is for God! 8

    The Healing Power of Faith 9

    A Poem for My Friend Called Terry 10

    Everyone Is Important to God and to Me 11

    My Nighttime Prayer 12

Part Two: Poetry of Politics 13

    I Will Defend You Any Day in Any Way 14

    Barbara's Court of Public Opinion 15

    Dare to Be Different 16

    I Want to Be a Faithful and True Supporter to You 17

    I Will Love and Support Your Presidency Forever 18

    Our President Will Fight On 19

    I Will Always Be on Your Side, Mr. President 20

    The Court of the Democrats and the Liberals 21

    Santa Says to Stop Picking on the Bloody President of the United States! 22

    Pardoning of the President by the Turkeys 24

Part Three: Poetry Especially for the President 25

    Thank You, Mr. President, for a Glorious Job So Far during Your Presidency 26

    The Ideal President 27

    You Are an Example of a Good American 28

    You Are Resilient and Courageous! 29

    You are resilient, Mr. President! 30

    "If I Were the Only One to Support You, I Would!" Cried the Republican Reindeer 31

    It Must Be Difficult to Run a Country 33

    To All My Friends, DT, BC, and MJ, I Am So, So Sorry! 34

    I Am So Proud of You in So Many Ways! 35

    I Have to Try 36

    Through the Eyes of a Republican Child 37

Part Four: Poetry, Poetry, and More Poetry! 39

    Writing Always Sustains Me! 40

    I Am Free to Be Me 41

    They Can Jolly Well Lump It! 42

    The Woes of a Shunned Fly 43

    The Wickedness of the Jealous 44

    What in the World Is Going on Here? 45

    The Balance Beam 46

    The Battle of My American Pocketbook; Dancing through My Misery 47

    The Swimming Party 48

    The Poetry Soldier 49

Part One: Poetry for God

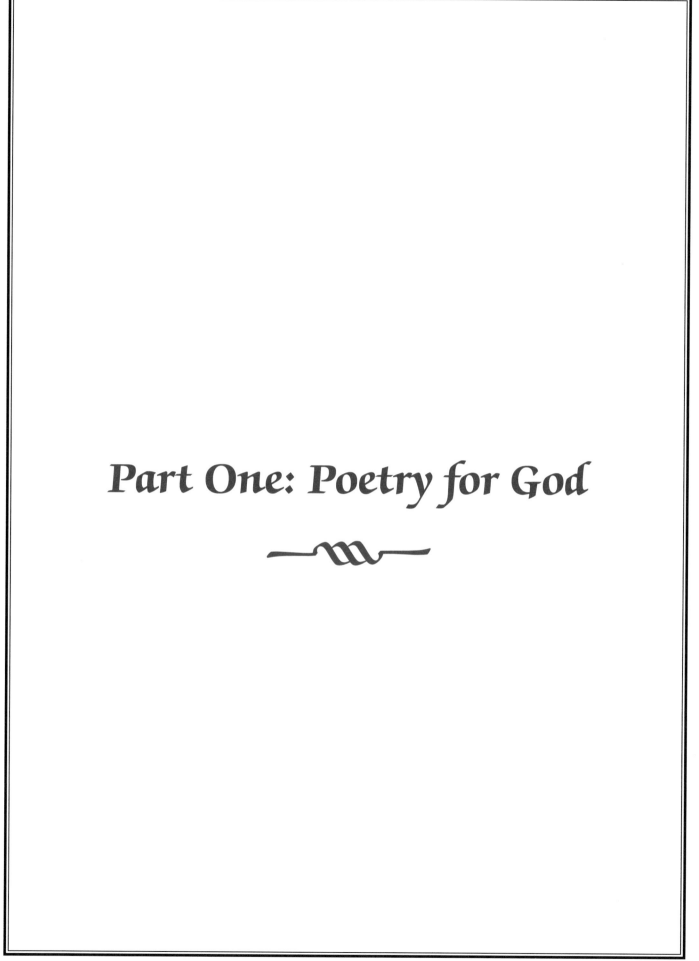

Jesus Set Us Free

If you are wondering today
why I am smiling with glee,
it is because today I am free;
Jesus has set me free!
I used to be a prisoner trapped in my solitary cell of sin and isolation within a prison of man's creation,
but now I know Jesus is my salvation without any question!
One day I can roam along the earth with him,
and I can sing songs of praise to him in person!
So just in case you have already forgotten just why I am smiling today,
I will tell you that I am saved today
because Jesus has set me free;
Jesus has set me free!
He has set you free today too from sin and despair,
so come ask him into your heart, why don't *you*?

The Day That God Wept upon the Earth

It was a difficult night, as God's own Son fought the battle, which we could never win on our own,
against our major enemy called *original sin*.
He saw that his Son bravely endured the harsh mockery, filled with unbearable hatred and excruciating
contempt and scorn,
while feeling troubled and forlorn.
The Father watched, while his most precious Son suffered lashings, beatings, and heavy bleeding.

The only thing worse was that our Father saw his one and only Son be put to death for crimes he never committed.
Though God could have helped his Son at any time,
both the Father and the Son sought to save us all from our misdeeds through crucifixion.
This happened at a time when the clouds were dark, and there were heavy rains (even though his Son's losses achieved our many gains)!

The tears from God's eyes were pouring onto the ground,
while he wept without a sound.
As he saw his most precious Son being treated like the most wretched human being,
anger rose in the clouds, and from there came a rumble of thunder.
All I can say is, "Thank you, Father, and thank you, Son, for with you, *all* things are possible!"
So this is how our world has been saved by the tears that you shed upon the earth,
while you showed us more love than we could ever deserve.

A Poem for My Savior and My King

I think of you constantly each and every day;
I think of you even when I *fail* to pray!
I think of you and how you *did* obey
your Father who sent you,
even when you knew that you were going to suffer *humiliation* and *excruciating* pain too!
While others may privately sing their praises to you,
and while some may join public worship in song, even if they cannot or better not sing along,
I think of how *great* you are and how you had to wait alone in the Garden of Gethsemane for your
accusers to arrive and begin the spectacle
that was even more dramatic and tragic than a play from Sophocles.
Not only do I thank you for saving me at Calvary through the greatest real-life drama and tragedy that
ever happened on earth,
but I am in awe of your love and your courage to follow through
on something no human ever could or would ever do!
I have to tell myself that if you could follow through with your Father's will for you no matter how
painful,
then I can do the same with my upcoming medical appointments,
even if I have fear and resentments
about the scary and painful roads that I must cross.
When I feel my fears and my tears come on,
I will use my faith to rely upon your power to save me from any tragic hour,
and I will think of you, my King, and I will follow you and your path unto the path of righteousness!

God Is Our Ray of Hope

We are living in a world filled with hopelessness and hatred, and this I know all too well,
but we *do* have a light of hope, however, that will save us from hell.
We have a loving God, who sent his Son to die for us on the cross
to not only save us from our sins
but also shine rays of optimism and hope
into the darkness of our failures and foibles.
Throughout our many trials and tribulations,
I believe that our *God* wants us to rely on *him*
and to trust that *he* will make things OK,
instead of ruining each other's day
with hatred, revenge, and just plain evil!
So when we begin to descend into emotional and spiritual darkness,
we need to remember that the God of healing *will* eventually *heal* our sicknesses,
and he *will* sort out our messes because
God is our ray of hope; he is our ray of hope!

How Did You Keep Quiet?

I was sitting under a hair dryer at the hairdresser,
and I was thinking about how you were
insulted so *badly* by your accusers!
I was wondering *how* you were able to *not* retaliate against those who were shouting insulting words of
blasphemy against you!
It must have hurt you so *badly* (since you *loved* them so *deeply* and were there to save us *all* from our sins
promptly)
to feel the sting of their annoying words of mockery and scorn;
you must have felt so depressed and so forlorn!
Yet through all this, you were able to stay strong, silent, and *sinless*,
where I would have screamed loads of profanity had it happened to me!
Your *holy, humble, loving* heart is packed with humility and generosity,
not to mention grace and forgiveness!
Possessing a spirit free from the traps of corruption and vengeance,
you were able to pray for those who mocked, condemned, and crucified you.
So the next time I get mocked or scorned by others so terribly and painfully, I will think of you, and I
will look up into the sky
and remember my *friend* and *Savior* who took away
my sins at Calvary, who spoke no words in reply to all the insults and to all the words so cruelly spoken
by the ignorant tyrant and the fools who were his allies!
Of all the greatest gifts you have given to us, your sacrificial love was demonstrated through silence and
through peace,
without any hostility toward anyone at all.

Beep! Judging Is for God!

I wish there were a type of answering machine
that would erase all words spoken out of judgment and hate.
Beep! Please leave a message for God, for he is the best one to judge!
Because God knows each and every heart,
he can tell the foolish from the smart
and the mean-spirited mastermind
from the soul who is generous and kind.
When I get angry at something someone says or does,
I should remind myself to call God's answering machine and leave a message
just so I can hear his soothing and reassuring message to me in reply on *my* spiritual answering machine.
"Beep! Please relax, Barb, because you know that I am God and that I will take care of everything! Have faith because you know that I will make everything all right!"

The Healing Power of Faith

During this pandemic, I discovered immediately
just how my faith in Jesus is helping me tremendously.
Sometimes I get overwhelmed to the point of becoming loose
and going out of control like a loose caboose!
When this does happen (which is quite frequently),
talking to God soothes the anxious soul within me
like a cup of cinnamon-flavored herbal tea
or a cup of warm milk chocolate–flavored cocoa that calms me ever so quickly.
Believing that there will be an end to this epidemic eventually,
and that we will win through God's victory,
is the best medicine for my troubled and afflicted spirit!

A Poem for My Friend Called Terry

I was sitting at the library today,
keeping to myself, as is my way,
and a friend of mine suddenly approached me,
complaining that he had been turned away from the local mall,
when he did nothing *whatsoever* at all;
he did nothing, *nothing, nothing* at all!
This happened before the pandemic took place,
and I thought to myself, "Oh, what a disgrace!"
At least I could give him some time and some company,
since I was very low on money!
He is my friend in trouble; he is my friend, you see.
He is my friend called Terry.
I thought to myself that as soon as I can, I will give Terry some money
because he is my friend in trouble, you see;
he is my *friend* called Terry.
Oh, Terry, I don't know where you are today,
but I sure hope that you are doing OK!

*E*veryone Is Important to God and to Me

Whether a person is in showbiz, politics, or law,
or whether he is just an average person like I am,
everyone is important to God, *everyone*!
No matter what choices a person has made in his or her life (fortunate or unfortunate choices they
may be),
everyone has worth to God for certainty
and also to me,
and for this reason,
even those in prison
have a right to be protected from the coronavirus
or any other disease that has befallen us!
Sadly, some people in our nation feel just the opposite; they believe that those who are inside a closet
called prison should not get released for their own protection and safety.
Instead, they think that they should stay
where they are, however dangerous it may be,
even though they were once a star formally!
I don't agree; all people should be protected equally because everyone is important to God and to me.
Everyone is important to God and to me!

My Nighttime Prayer

As I lie in bed at night, I think of all my wishes and prayers for this world, and by

far, the one that continues to dominate

my precious moment to meditate

is how much I would like the sick hate

that permeates and radiates

from the political debates

of today and then some

to be replaced with mutual respect and courtesy that will never go away!

I really hope that I can see,

before I escape this place of misery,

a newfound love for others that will transform society

into a place of love for God and a love for man permanently.

Part Two: Poetry of Politics

I Will Defend You Any Day in Any Way

No matter what I read or hear about you online or in the press, I will always be here to defend you, *yes, yes, yes*!

For you are my favorite president,

and you have motivated my activism without precedent!

Because you have defended our nation with courage and with zest,

performing well under many a test,

it is no wonder, then, that I think *you* are the *best*!

You have served your term (and your next term too)

with tenacity and courage too,

much better than others in your situation would do!

I am here, therefore, to say that I *will* defend you *any day in any way*,

because I am so grateful to you for your loyalty to our country and to your constituents,

and I will not listen or pay attention to the words of those who refuse to give you the credit and honor that you are due;

the words from the hateful and the ignorant will drop from my mind like rain that tumbles down from the sky,

and if they ask me, "*Why, why, why?*"

I will reply, "It is because I want to and also because I take orders from the holy One in the sky!"

Barbara's Court of Public Opinion

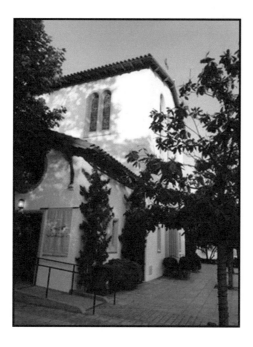

So many false reports and allegations were made against you,
some of which were very harmful and hurtful too!
Your critics should have seen the righteous actions you performed out of love for this country.
When they failed to do so, it just made me so very angry!
You were treated like you were some unwanted bug or fly,
one that they could just brush away
and to which they would say, "Just leave me alone! You are a pain in the a . . ."
They didn't *care* about the pain and the shame that they caused you and your family.
Instead, they continued to simply
criticize
and to politicize,
when they should have shown you the benefit of the doubt, the fairness, and the love that would have
buffered the many bitter cruel insults and injustices that were thrown against you.
Since they didn't do this for you, I will do it myself.

1. You and your family are loved and adored by Barbara's court of public opinion
2. You are not guilty of any allegation or crime
3. You are the best president we have ever had
4. You are a special human being with lots of potential
5. God loves you, and so do I
6. I admire you, and I always will

President Donald Trump and First Family

Dare to Be Different

We should be living in an atmosphere
where it should be absolutely clear
that everyone's opinion *does* matter
and *not just* the opinions of those who are in power,
who seem to be in control of the hour!
When our country caves into the whims of the intolerant
to the point where even the president cannot say what he thinks or feels without consequence,
when he cannot protect our country or do his job
because of those who just want their own way and no one else's,
when we fail to dare to be different from the conformist crowd in power,
I fear for our nation's well-being!
For the USA is *not* a country of conformists, communists, and socialists.
The USA is a country filled with individuals who dare to be different and who dare to stand up for their country!
Our country will not surrender to socialism, communism, or the whims of an overpowerful abusive Congress who is abusing their power because they cannot accept the reality or the success of a new and popular president who is superior to them!
I say we dare to be different and make our thoughts known
and allow others to do the same;
otherwise, we will bring shame to the vision that our forefathers had when they wrote the Constitution.
Dare to be different is what I say.
Dare to be different!
Dare to be different!

I Want to Be a Faithful and True Supporter to You

There has never been a president like you
in quite some time who has cared for our country so deeply,
and because of this, I want to be a faithful and true supporter to you!
There has never been a president like you
who has done what he promised for our nation immediately,
and for this, I want to be a faithful and true supporter to you!
There has never been a president like you who has been so faithful and compassionate to all Americans,
even to those who would gladly throw you under the bus,
and for this, I want to be a faithful and true supporter to you!
There has never been an honest and more honorable president in a long time like you,
and for this, I want to be a faithful and true supporter to you!
You are someone who has stood up for the common man and for righteous principles,
and for this, I want to be a faithful and true supporter to you!
You may be going through an unjust impeachment inquiry right now,
but you will soon win victory over your false accusers with a mighty blow,
and for this, I want to be a faithful and true supporter to you.
I want to be a faithful and true supporter to you!

I Will Love and Support Your Presidency Forever

Through your presidency, you have suffered through many storms and many strong waves too,
yet you have managed to remain courageous and brave without ever becoming blue.
Impeachment trials never brought you down, nor did terrible articles about you in the press
ever take away your success.
Anyone might have quit or resigned,
but you emerged with a confidence fine.
You never gave up, nor will you ever surrender yourself to fear or despair,
and I just *know* that you will guide us through this pandemic,
and this will be one of your accomplishments most *epic*!
I will not fear, for
I know that the presence of God is here
through your capable hands and leadership,
which is *not* a dictatorship!
For this, and for many other reasons, I want you to know that I will always love and support you
and your presidency too!

Our President Will Fight On

If there is one thing I know, and this is something that I have known all along,
it's that our president will fight on,
in spite of what his enemies do!
He will fight on for his country, if he has to sue, sue, sue, and *sue*!
Not only will my president survive the impeachment, but his *many* supporters will fight on for him for as
long as it takes!
Yes, Mr. President, we, your faithful followers, *will fight* for *you*
because we know the love for your country and the American people that is in your heart so genuine and
true,
and there has not been anyone like you!

I Will Always Be on Your Side, Mr. President

There are so many subjects that I could write about,
some of which make me angry and pout,
but you are not one of them, Mr. President.
You are not one of them!
I believe that God has blessed me with a gift for writing,
because writing to me is fun and exciting
and writing to defend you is a *special honor,*
and it is a *privilege* too,
for I have never admired any president like I have you.
Because you are a strong leader and you are genuine too,
I will always keep writing for you,
and I want you to know, Mr. President, that I will always be on your side.
I will always be on your side.
Nothing matters more than our national security
and the proper running of our country,
but the powers that be just want to be Trump-free!
They want this so that they can force people to bow to their whims!
Some may believe you are a dictator,
but it is the political party that opposes you
that is totalitarian and the true police state.
If you do not do what they say or believe in,
they will make a price for you to pay on social media, censorship, or even libel or slander.
So I want you to know that *I will always be on your side, Mr. President*; I will always be on your side!

The Court of the Democrats and the Liberals

If you want freedom of speech and tolerance of dissension,
don't go to the court of the democrats and the liberals!
If you want to feel free and safe in this country,
don't go to the court of the democrats and the liberals!
If you want a fair and just trial for everyone and anyone,
don't go to the courts of the democrats and the liberals!
If you want a baby-safe nation and a traditional marriage in our country,
don't go to the courts of the democrats and the liberals!
If you want a God-loving country,
don't go to the courts of the democrats and the liberals!
If you want to have a happy peaceful nation,
flee from the courts of the democrats and the liberals!

Santa Says to Stop Picking on the Bloody President of the United States!

I am enjoying my much needed break
on the island of Santa Catalina
that I take before the rush of Christmas delivery begins.
I try not to listen to the news as much,
but I still like to stay in touch,
and I cannot understand why it seems to me that everyone picks on this poor president!
The president of the United States is simply trying to lead your country
to safety and prosperity,
but his foes try to emotionally tie his hands behind his back and prevent him from doing what he feels is
right
because his courage to change things for the better in this country is something they lack!
I just cannot sit and watch this poor bloody president who does so much for his country continue to be
humiliated while all his foes just smirk or complain!
So all I have to say to the world now is, *"Stop picking on the bloody president of the United States!"*

Pardoning of the President by the Turkeys

Gobble! Gobble! Gobble!
Thank you so much for pardoning us!
We hate that you constantly get thrown under the bus
by those who do not understand you!
Gobble! Gobble! Gobble!
We think that your foes should pardon you on the double!
Gobble! Gobble! Gobble!
Life is too short to be wasted on hatred and negativity,
especially when others criticize you needlessly
during your excellent presidency!
Gobble! Gobble! Gobble!
If the fools in the government do not pardon you on the double,
we will disappear so there won't be any of us around to cook on this next Christmas Day.
Gobble! Gobble! Gobble!
Today is now called Turkey Proclamation Day, and we demand that the hateful treatment of our
president go away by this Christmas Day!

Part Three: Poetry Especially for the President

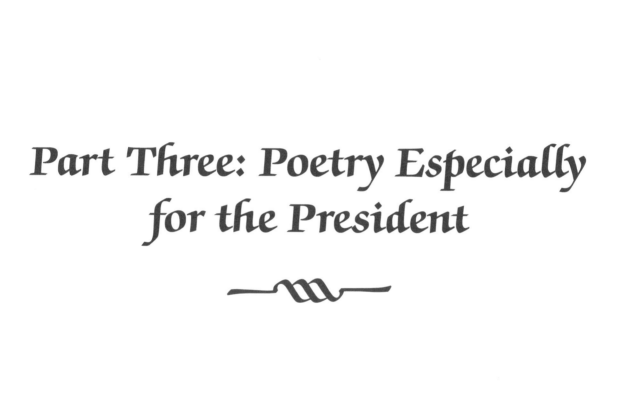

Thank You, Mr. President, for a Glorious Job So Far during Your Presidency

I cannot say enough once again
that I think that you are a great man!
You have persevered through so much pain,
yet you always got up, *got up, got up again*!
You had many opponents who just wanted to destroy you, and they wanted to humiliate you too,
but you never gave into their ferocious attempts; not once did their vicious ploys succeed!
You came out the victor! Yes, indeed!
You have made (and will *continue* to make) the US a winning economy,
which is why many (including me)
praise you so highly
for all that you have done so far during your presidency!
*So thank you, again, thank you, Mr. President, for you have been a blessing to me
and to this country!*

The Ideal President

The ideal president of a country is one who balances power with compromise.
The ideal president of a country does what he thinks is wise,
and he looks up to the God who is in the skies
for guidance in all his affairs.
Regardless of those around him who oppose God and his plans,
the ideal president is one who will not bow to any oppression that puts the country in danger.
The ideal president will take care of his country first before anything else.
The ideal president will listen to others' opinions but will ultimately decide on his own what the best course of action is.
The ideal president will love all his people regardless of what they say or do.
For all these reasons, I say that you, President Trump, are our *ideal* president
because you are everything and more without precedent!

You Are an Example of a Good American

You are an example of a good American because:

1. You value patriotism and the sacrifice of those who have gone before
2. You value the lives and the safety of both those who and who are not your supporters
3. You value the rights of all Americans regardless of who they may be
4. You are not afraid to lead our country into victory
5. You seek to find ways to keep jobs in the US
6. You try to find the best deal for insurance recipients without taking advantage of anyone
Finally, you are an example of a good American

because there is no question that you love the US with all your heart!

You Are Resilient and Courageous!

Even though I have made many mistakes,
and I have misjudged a few,
I must pick myself up again
and be resilient too.
So many times I have heard it said
that, when one goes through periods we dread,
or periods when one would rather hide on their own instead,
it is so important to get up and face the world
again, after suffering shame, humiliation, and bitter pain.
It has been said by Eleanor Roosevelt that one cannot be made to feel inferior without their consent,
so it is now the time for me to become courageous and to let go of all fear and resentment.
For life is too short to be anything less than courageous and resilient.

You are resilient, Mr. President!

Do not forget that!

"If I Were the Only One to Support You, I Would!" Cried the Republican Reindeer

"If I were the only one to support you, I would!" cried the Republican Reindeer.

"If I were the only one to wave at you from within an unsupportive crowd, I would!" cried the Republican Reindeer.

"If I were the only one to vote for you, I would!" cried the Republican Reindeer.

"If I were the only one to honor you, I would!" cried the Republican Reindeer.

"If I were the only one to write poems for you, I would!" cried the Republican Reindeer.

"If I were the only human around, I would sing for you!" cried the Republican Reindeer.

"If I were the only one to vote for you, I would, but since I'm not human, my friend Barbara, who is also Republican, will do it for me!" cried the Republican Reindeer.

<<Missing Image>>

"Ho, ho, ho!" says Santa Claus. "I'm going to make President Trump president again in 2020!"

It Must Be Difficult to Run a Country

Today I look at the leaders from different parts of the world,
and I think to myself, "It must be so hard to run a country!"
It is especially more complicated if you are kind and generous,
not to mention tender and sensitive.
You have to be prepared for others to not like you or to be disappointed with you as president,
because there is no such thing as a perfect president, and as hard as one works to try to serve all the
people in one's country and to make them all happy,
there is always going to be someone who will not go along with your policies,
and you have to be strong enough to rise above any hatred or resentments or tears and disappointments
that time in the White House will surely bring!
You have to be *strong* and *assertive* enough to do what is best for our country even when your enemies
both inside and outside of your country mock you and humiliate you with scathing words of contempt
and ridicule
with some of these people behaving like they never even went to high school!
It is not easy being president, this I know, and I am so glad that it is you rather than me,
because you are handling things wonderfully to me!

To All My Friends, DT, BC, and MJ, I Am So, So Sorry!

<<Missing Image>>

Even if you are the only ones who will see this poem, it doesn't matter to me,
because I need to do something to let you know how *sorry* I am
for all that has been said and reported about you all in the public arena!
All of you are kind and loving people too,
so why should any people believe less than that about all of you?
Sadly, we live in a hate-filled world where even our poor president cannot escape wrongful judgment and condemnation
and even *impeachment* in Washington!
I tell you that I get so down that I really wish that I could escape this world and be with my family in heaven,
but I know that my God has a plan for me down here to continue growing in him
and to fight against injustice and hatred wherever I am,
so I will wait until it is my time to meet Jesus!
In the meantime, please know how *so, so sorry* I am for the cruel treatment that all of you have endured,
because I will always love and admire all of you,
in spite of what has been spoken of or has been written about you.

I Am So Proud of You in So Many Ways!

I am *so* proud of you in *so* many ways!

1. You don't give in to pessimism or despair.
2. You lead with firm authority, yet you also run our country with reassuring words of hope and courage.
3. You bravely take on your foes in debates.
4. You aren't afraid of anything or anyone.
5. You are *proudly* a president for *God*!
6. You are *not* nor will you *ever* be a pushover!

I Have to Try

At times it seems like a long shot to bring peace to the world, but I have to try!
At times it seems impossible to bring justice and mercy into our world, but I have to try!
At times it seems impossible to publish poetry that will mean something to anybody, but I have to try!
At times I don't always feel like I can help anybody with my words and my poetry,
but I have to try no matter how challenging the obstacles in my life may be.
I have to try!
I have to try!
I really want to show love to everybody,
and I want to give hope to the downtrodden and the rejected of this world because that is what my Lord
did for me!
I know that he saved me at Calvary,
and then he pursued me until he got me!
So I have to try!
I have to try!

Through the Eyes of a Republican Child

Today I went to the mall, and I went to a store called Santa's Door.
Before I entered, I thought a lot about what I would ask him for.
I thought that perhaps I should ask Santa to give me a new neighbor next door,
one who would not tease or make fun of me anymore,
but when I approached Santa and his tree,
I suddenly remembered my mother's misery.
I realized that what I really *wanted* was for my mother to be happy
because she is so important to me!
I love her so *deeply*
that it truly, truly *pains* me
to see her so distressed and unhappy,
so I asked Santa to put the president out of his misery
and stop this stupid impeachment
of our favorite president!
My wish was granted, and I am happy
to report that that my mom is definitely
glad and that she is no longer unhappy.

Part Four: Poetry, Poetry, and More Poetry!

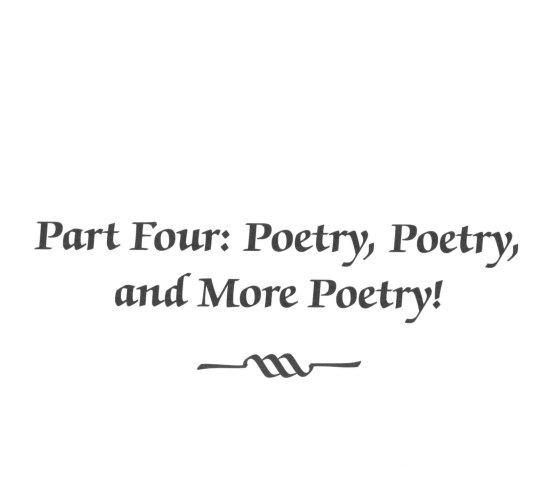

Writing Always Sustains Me!

I am now considering surgery to remove my gallbladder with great trepidation, and
I am facing upcoming dental work, which I completely dread,
and sometimes I wish I were dead,
but writing will sustain me in the end
because writing *always* sustains me!
I will continue to live my life fully,
in spite of the heavy grieving that has come upon me
because writing will sustain me;
writing *always* sustains me!
It seems like no matter what celebrity mortality or pandemic wraps itself around our country,
I cannot linger long in misery
because writing sustains me;
writing *always* sustains me!
So as long as I live,
I will continue to write,
for writing sustains me;
writing will *always* sustain me!

I Am Free to Be Me

I miss being in a place that is not so far away,
yet when I go there, I feel free,
free to be me!
Deep within the Catalina Island Conservancy,
where buffalo abound and bushes and trees,
it truly brings one's woes to its knees!
I miss sitting on a bench by the blue waters of Avalon,
indulging in a waffle ice cream cone,
licking the sweet chocolate sauce off of my fingers,
and feeding bits of my cone to local critters.
I think to myself that here, even though I feel alone,
I am not truly alone.
How I miss being on Catalina Island,
my closest thing to paradise in this land,
because here I am free to be me;
I am free to be me!

They Can Jolly Well Lump It!

I once had a friend who told me that if someone didn't like me for who I was, he or she could jolly well
lump it!
I would like to give this same advice to you,
because it has helped me, and I think it will help you too!
To me, you have nothing to hide, and you have nothing to prove,
and besides, many of Americans are so proud of you, and we love you too!
Although we think that you are a wonderful president, unfortunately,
many choose to disagree with us, and I know that so many seek to humiliate you through various ways
and means,
especially with this confounded impeachment policy,
so with this poem, I do declare proudly
that I am *not* one of your many critics because I am on your side *always*, and
I will *always* be on your side!
More importantly, I consider you a friend whom I haven't met yet,
and I want you to know that I love and admire you with all my heart,
and those who find fault with that
can jolly well *lump it*!

The Woes of a Shunned Fly

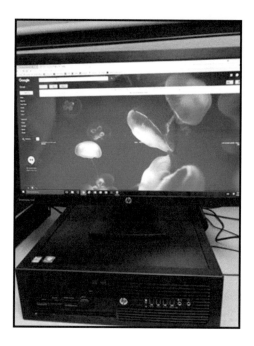

I have to fly around to get my food,
and my life as a fly is *not* easy!
All day long, we hear, *"Shoo, fly, shoo!"*
as we are continually brushed away, while seeking affection through human contact.
There seems to be no end to the *lack* of tact
that we receive from swatters, hands, or "Go away, fly!" demands we get,
and now the blasted Congress is doing the same thing to your president of the United States through
this impeachment inquiry!
So thank you, liberals; I will no longer complain about my life as a shunned fly,
because I'd rather be me than be the victim of an *unjust* impeachment inquiry!

The Wickedness of the Jealous

There are so many people who are jealous of
those who appear to be more successful in life than the average person,
whether they be politicians, athletes, movie stars, or anyone who is famous.
Those people who are jealous have lost sight of what is important in life,
and they want things to be given to them without any cost, including *freedom*.
However, the worst of the jealous ones seem to be those politicians who are greedy, selfish, and petty and
who don't deserve their seats in government,
and it is these people today who seek without regret the impeachment of a sitting president.
For some reason, although he has done nothing wrong,
the jealous love to sing the guilty's song!
If truth be told, *we should impeach these foolish childish incompetents in our Congress*
who are undeserving of our respect and admiration;
we should be impeaching those people in Congress who are extremely jealous
of our president who is now in power,
who are otherwise called
stupid jealous liberals!

What in the World Is Going on Here?

I cannot believe what is going on in the world today;
the love for fairness in our legal system and in the media has gone away!
Anyone who claims they have been attacked or assaulted, whether true or not,
can come before a court and *sue, sue, sue*!
I thought that there was a provision within our Constitution to protect against double jeopardy,
where people cannot be tried twice for the same crime!
These days, if you have the money and the fame and the power, and you hate someone,
you can easily destroy a person's life and reputation!
Our forefathers who sought to protect the innocent from undeserved incarceration
would roll over in their graves if they saw how innocent people get destroyed before they get convicted!
The creators of our Constitution would be shocked and horrified if they saw today
how a person's life can be taken away,
just because they are accused of something in the media or in the entertainment news
prior to the benefit of a fair, impartial, and unbiased trial!
When I look at how our freedoms have been abused in order that some may profit unfairly at someone
else's incarceration or another's unnecessary impeachment,
I just have to raise my hands and cry,
"What in the world is going on here?"

The Balance Beam

I took a class in gymnastics once
as part of my PE course,
which I needed for my high school graduation.
No way was I any good by any stretch of the imagination!
As I made my way along the narrow plank of wood,
I saw that there was nothing below the darn plank
to protect me from cutting or scraping myself easily,
should I fall off that stupid balance beam!
I knew that I had no choice other than to slowly make my way forward,
and also backward,
along the slippery brown beam of wood
doing the very best that I could.
Today many years later, I feel sometimes we are walking on a spiritual and moral balance beam, which
requires continually walking along the straight and the narrow to avoid a fall, while not knowing what
one day will bring or the morrow.
Nevertheless, even if I want to do other things to let off steam,
I will nevertheless continue to persevere on my walk along the balance beam,
in pursuit of the American dream.

The Battle of My American Pocketbook; Dancing through My Misery

Hi, everybody! I am here for you to see
dancing through my misery!
I have no money within my body
because my owner spends every penny
to *publish, publish, publish* like crazy!
I cannot feel any dollar or quarter,
because it is all spent in less than an hour!
Oh, how I wish I were human, so I could taste the food that humans taste,
but I can only hold money or that which is left within me
because I am a pocketbook, and this makes me crazy!
Since I cannot taste any money as it departs so quickly,
I simply must dance through my misery;
I must dance through my misery!

The Swimming Party

While I went out to sea for my fifty-fifth birthday,
I saw some dolphins come up to me,
as if they were trying to wish me a happy birthday.
One of these playful mammals showed their
vanilla-colored stomachs to me,
as they splashed and dove into the cool blue saltwater so gracefully.
I wished I could join their swimming party
and savor the cold freshness of the blue sea that was in front of me!

The Poetry Soldier

I may not be a good-looking celebrity,
and I may be too old to join the military;
I may not be the girl you want to sleep with desperately,
nor may I be someone you want to marry.
But this advantage I do carry:
I can fight for others through my poetry,
for I am the poetry soldier;
I am the poetry soldier!
Though many shoot verbal or written swords at the public figure,
whether he or she is a celebrity or a political leader,
I will carry my shield of words and allusions
created in my imagination for him or her,
and I will become the poetry soldier;
I *will* defend other people's honor,
for I am the poetry soldier.
I am the poetry soldier!

Printed in the United States
by Baker & Taylor Publisher Services